ESSENTIAL GUIDE TO SELLING & BUYING REAL ESTATE

A Real Estate Broker's Inside Secrets to Save You Money

Glen Anthony Gomez

ISBN: 1546814329
ISBN 13: 9781546814320

INTRODUCTION

I started in real estate in 1999, buying and flipping properties for a profit. I worked a full-time job—perhaps fifty to fifty-five hours per week—in medical-device sales. I had to deal with hospital administrators, physicians, insurance companies, and many other decision makers. Yes, it was a kiss-ass job. I had to be in the hospital at 7:00 a.m., and normally my day was finished at around 8:00 p.m. Sometimes I worked right through to the next day. My work hours depended on the surgical schedule and the particular schedule of the surgeon.

I've always wanted to help people. Helping complete strangers with their health issues was the most rewarding feeling I have ever experienced. Helping people make what is often the most important investment of their lives—buying or selling a home—is also extremely rewarding.

Since I had to work around the surgeons' schedules in my medical-sales job, my schedule had to be somewhat flexible. I didn't have to be in the office all day. One advantage to these flexible, if long, hours was the time I found between appointments to devote to other interests—like real estate. I'd always wanted to invest in real estate. I used to watch those late-night real estate investment infomercials and spent a lot of money teaching myself about the subject.

No matter what anybody tells you, it takes money to invest in real estate. This "no money down" or "you don't need money to buy and sell real estate for a profit" business is all a bucket of you know what.

I finally purchased my investment. I will go into my first investment in the investment chapter. But I will tell you now that investing in real estate for the first time can be a major headache when going it on your own for the first time.

You may be wondering if I made any money buying and selling real estate. The answer is yes and no.

I retired from medical sales to devote all my efforts to real estate. Wow. What a crazy business. Real estate can be fun, but most of the time, it's frustrating. There are a lot of moving parts, and if you don't know this, you are guaranteed to get ripped off.

I was ripped off more often than I realized. It wasn't until I became seasoned in dealing with so-called real estate professionals that I learned how to protect myself.

Many professionals only want to make money. They don't care about you or your needs.

In writing this book, I'm hoping to share important knowledge with you so you won't make the same mistakes I did.

PREFACE

I was inspired to write this book after attending a real estate transaction that went chaotic.

Most people make a real estate transaction only every five to ten years and don't clearly understand all that goes into the transaction.

I have seen very smooth transactions and a lot of hell-raising transaction. I am hoping you will better understand the process of a real estate transaction, including investing, selling, buying, and dealing with lenders and title companies.

There are a lot of moving parts involved within a real estate transaction, and if you are not aware of them, you will be ripped off and taken advantage of.

I want to help you have the basic understanding of all that goes on behind a real estate transaction. Perhaps you will share this book with your family and friends and allow them to save some money too.

After all, real estate is probably your biggest investment other than an automobile purchase.

Everyone knows how to bargain for a car, but how many out there know how to bargain when dealing with their biggest life investment?

I will share with you my experience and expertise in real estate transaction, and hopefully you will gain at least one important idea that could help you.

To schedule public seminars, please contact us at info@joystarr.com. or visit joystarr.com for more information about Joystar Realty Group

I dedicate this book to my wife, entire family, and the Joystar team.

REAL ESTATE AGENTS

When I was flipping real estate properties, I had to use Realtors. For the most part, it was a good experience until I realized I was the one doing all the work. So why was I paying a real estate agent just to place my property on the MLS?

I recall one not-so-good experience with a Realtor. I'd asked for the HUD, the closing statement that shows all the fees, commission, taxes, and government recording fees. I explained to everyone that I would not sign until I reviewed the HUD. I was told that the buyer had already signed and the money was ready to be wired into my account. I repeated, "I will not sign until I review the HUD."

Finally, I received the HUD closing documents and saw why the agent and title company hadn't wanted me to see the HUD Document

On the HUD document, the real estate agent was charging me 10 percent, and the buyer's agent was getting 2 percent. That meant I would be paying a total of 12 percent commission.

Are you ready to hear what the title company was charging me? Here it goes: the title-service fee was $2,200, the notary fees $175, the FedEx fees $100, the wiring fees $120, the abstract fees $300, and the storage fees $60. I could go on and on. This entire transaction was intended to milk as much from me as possible.

I told everyone that I would not be signing this HUD closing disclosure due to the amount of commission and fees.

The agent didn't get paid. However, I did pay the buyer's agent the 2 percent, and I was able to reduce the title-company fees.

If I didn't know better, I would have gotten ripped off big time. I trusted the Realtor. He made all the arrangements with the title company. I almost thought I was good to go. They were thinking I would sign because the money was ready to be wired into my bank account. They tried to play on my greed. Yeah, send the money. I don't think so.

After this experience I told my wife that I was going to get my real estate license, and so I did.

Now I have my real estate license and am working full time in this business. I guess, like any type of business, it can be cutthroat. When I had to hang my license with a real estate company, it was all about the money.

These big-box companies take most of your commission plus all those additional franchise, royalty, transaction, and other fees. I was working just to make money for the broker.

We live in a technology generation. I am going to make a statement that will shock you: these big-box companies will be out of business in the very near future.

Why? Technology. Everyone has a computer and can search the Internet. Most buyers are increasingly locating homes before the agents find them by using the Internet. Before long, 99 percent of buyers and renters will search the Internet to buy or rent a home.

The big Internet websites, such as Zillow, Realtor.com, Trulia, Hubzu, and Nationstar, along with banks, will be selling real estate if they're not already doing so.

Nevertheless, there's a catch to these Internet sellers: their goal is to make as much money as possible from you, so I don't see the real estate agent being replaced any time soon.

There are too many moving parts. You want a professional handling your transaction. It's your biggest investment, and you want the communication skills and other capabilities of a professional to handle any problem that comes along.

Here are the reasons why you need a professional Realtor to handle your biggest investment:

1. They know the business. You want someone who has the necessary knowledge to handle your biggest investment and can resolve any issue that comes along.
2. Can you really trust anyone who is working offshore or in another state? You need someone who is familiar with your market area.
3. A Realtor knows how to prepare a contract. A lot of people don't understand the minute they sign a contract, it's legally binding. It's a legal contract, and if anyone defaults, the result could mean facing a judge and losing money.
4. A Realtor can make all the arrangements with a licensed home inspector. At my firm we compose a list of home inspectors whom we have used and had good results with and invite our clients to call each home inspector on the list to determine which one is the best match for them.
5. A Realtor can perform a professional competitive market analysis if you are buying or

selling a property. A professional competitive market analysis is one of the most important components in a real estate transaction. Here is why: you may be a buyer and want to submit an offer, and the offer exceeds the fair market values of homes that are similar. Most likely the home wouldn't appraise for your offer amount. And if your agent didn't prepare an appraisal contingency, you could be in a lot of trouble. Always review the competitive market analysis with your Realtor. Don't worry if the seller demands the list price, and the comparables don't support it. Just look for another property.

Sellers typically want the most for their property. I can't blame a seller for that. It's only human nature to get the most money possible. I own a 1997 Nissan and was offered $1,000 for it. I said, "No way, Jose. That car is worth at least ten times that amount."

But I was not being realistic. I know the true price for this car is about $300–$800; however, the car means a lot to me. It was my father's old car, and I am not planning to sell it anyway. My intention is to restore it.

My point is that if you are selling, you must be realistic on your sale price. If you have the price too high, you are not going to see any buyers. Your property will just sit on the market for a long time. Plus when most agents see it listed for a long time, they will think that there's a major issue with the property and will not waste their time showing it.

Your real estate agent should perform a professional competitive market analysis on your property. It should include recently sold properties that are similar to yours. Look only at properties that were sold within ninety days and are within one mile. Most likely these properties are what an appraiser would look at. Your buyer would likely be financing, so a good agent would price the home properly so you could get the maximum dollars for your property.

6. You need a real estate agent to make arrangement for the showings of your property. This needs to fit around your schedule. My firm schedules appointments where we have multiple showings on the same day. We have families waiting outside the door to view the property. This is not a gimmick but a way to show that this property will not last long on the market. We usually receive three to four good, solid offers the same week.

7. You need a real estate agent to handle the appraisal. A good agent would have already

submitted the purchase agreement along with the comparables to the appraisal company.

The appraisal is a real deal killer. A good agent could erase this key factor.

8. For the closing, a Realtor makes all the necessary arrangements with the title company and reviews the closing documents for any inaccuracies.

I started as a real estate, as do 100 percent of the brokers in this business. I learned about how to set up a firm and be completive. I learned from being a typical one-off buyer to selling fifteen properties a year.

There are real estate agents in every corner. They may be friends or family members. Remember the agent who wanted to charge me 10 percent commission? He was my golf buddy!

I do not recommend using a friend or family member unless it's your spouse, and you better use your spouse. But seriously, try to stay away from a friend or a second cousin. This is business and considered a business transaction. There is a lot of personal information that may be sensitive.

Find a professional real estate agent who is an expert to handle your needs. If you are buying, selling, or investing real estate, surround yourself with expertise. This is a big investment.

You need someone that understands your market area, pricing, lending, and dealing with title companies. It's not that you need a professional having twenty years of experience. I have an agent with one year of experience and heading to be one of my best producing agents. He has passion and the knowledge, plus he educates himself on the necessary areas.

The majority of agents wouldn't educate themselves. For the most part, real estate schools only instruct a candidate how to pass the state exam and not how to conduct real estate business. The local realtor board offers many courses ranging from financing to foreign national investors. Ninety percent of real estate agents don't take any of these classes. I could never figure this one out. Our firm has monthly webinars on such topics as doing a competitive market analysis, FHA versus conventional financing, title companies' fees, and contracts. At least once a month, we get into it.

Before I was a not real estate agent, I looked for advice from friends. Following their directions, I thought I could do it all on my own. I was wrong. As stated above, look for an expert, interview agents, and don't always go to a big-box agency. You end up spending more due to all those additional fees, and I will tell you the agent who is acting on your behalf will not pay those additional fees. This is coming out of your pocket.

Appearances Matter

When you interview a real estate agent to buy or sell your property, look at how they dress. Are they dressed professionally?

Don't laugh, but look at the type of car they are driving. Is the car clean or dirty? Is the car blowing smoke and barely operating? One of my customers told me that he wouldn't use a particular agent because of the type of car he was driving. This customer explained that the car was a mess, and the agent himself was sloppy. I hadn't realized that customers look at the entire picture of a person, and the car is image of that person. Since then I kept my car clean even though I drive a seven-year-old car.

Is the agent you are interviewing pushing you to sign, sign, sign? Run, run, run!

Your biggest investment is on the line here. You don't want to work with pushy used car salesperson. You want someone that is patient and listens to you. You are running the show, not the agent. The agent is there as an expert and for advice.

When you go to see your doctor, that physician listens to you to find out the best solution for your illness. It should be the same when picking a real estate agent.

You shop for someone to do your landscaping, taxes, legal needs, pool care, and so forth. If they are not performing up to the task, guess what? "You are fired!"

Over my real estate venture, I have hire and fired more people than Mr. Trump.

Hire a real estate agent who understands that every property is different. No property is the same. They are unique in every way, and a good agent completely understands this.

Would I charge a 6 percent commission on a sale of a property where the seller is only making a few hundred dollars? Of course not. If there is not a lot of margin or equity, a good agent will know how to structure the transaction where there's a happy client. It's your money. Why should you give your hard-earned money to someone who wouldn't understand your needs? Yes, in some cases a 6 percent commission is due based on the property's condition or location, which amounts to more work for the agent.

I once had a buyer who needed to sell. Her daughter worked for one of those big-box companies, and she couldn't give her the listing due to all those mandatory fees. Going into it I didn't think that I would get the listing, but I listened to her and worked out a winning solution for her because I listened to her. Every transaction is unique. Use a professional agent who understands this. This is one of the most important pieces of advice I could give. This holds true if you are buying. Do you really want an agent to show you properties that you don't like or that tries to steer you into neighborhoods not to your liking? You need to hire an agent who listens and understands that every person is unique and is not all about the money.

Do you need a full-time real estate agent working for you? This again depends on the agent. We have part-time agents who are producing more than the full-time agents. This will be up to you. If you are buying and selling, you want to make sure that agent is answering the calls, making appointments, arranging scheduling of the inspection, appraisal, closing details, and most importantly is reachable.

Real Estate Agent or Real Estate Broker

Is it better to use a real estate broker or an agent? Once again this depends on the agent and broker. A good agent could handle and do a better job than a broker. Big-box brokers typically stay in the office all day managing. They may not have enough time to take care of your needs. The only benefit of using the broker is reducing some of those added fees. If you're considering working with a broker, make sure he or she has enough time to handle your needs.

Since I am a broker, I set aside enough time to manage my clients' transactions, which is the reason why we don't need one hundred real estate agents. Most brokers want more agents because it's all about the numbers: "more agents more transactions." I say, more agents more headaches. I like a family-size atmosphere, so if an agent needs to ask a question, he or she can always reach out to me or to a team leader. This is important if you are buying or selling. You want that personal touch and caring. If you go to the doctor, you want to see the same doctor. It's the same in the real estate business. A personal touch is always the best approach, as I learned over the years. These big-box companies don't have the time to review your contract before it becomes executed. You want to make sure your contract is reviewed by an expert and by management. A contract is binding and could become a legal matter.

Chapter Summary
Carefully choose an expert—a true professional—to handle your transaction.

Some good agents may charge a retainer fee. This is OK because this could be an indication they will get the work done correctly. In most states most agents charge a retainer fee. Just be careful to screen them well. Ask if this retainer will be credited back to you at the closing.

Relax. After reading this chapter, you will be able to pick out the good agents. Overall most agents are honest. However, there are many details attached to real estate, so make sure the agent you are working with is an expert in that area.

Ask yourself, is this person an expert for my needs? Does he or she understand the unique nature of real estate? Does this person handle himself or herself professionally? Does this agent listen to me, understand my goals, appreciate that I am running the show? Am I being pushed to sign? Is this agent reachable? Does this agent understand the culture of financing? Does this agent know how to interpret a closing statement in my best interest? Is the agent in tune with the latest updates and trends in the market? Can this agent perform a comparison market analysis? Can I trust this agent to handle my transaction?

In my opinion it doesn't matter how many transactions an agent had performed. To me if they can't give you that personal touch, it doesn't make difference. A rookie agent may do a better job than a seasoned agent. A seasoned agent may just be collecting inventory or listings and not marketing your property if you are selling. If you are buying, look for an agent who understands your likes and dislikes. In my first meeting with a buyer, I will interview him or her and allow him or her to interview me. Ninety-nine percent of the time, I will pick out the home they end up buying or renting. You need to find this ability in your agent. This is the only way it will work. Your agent needs to be on the same level as you.

Most agents don't like working with renters because it's harder and provides less commission, and renters usually tend to have only bad to fair credit. When we work with renters, we increase their credit score, so it's an easier task to find a rental. If you are a homeowner, would you rent your hard-earned investment home to a candidate with a credit score of 550 or to one with a score of 700?

We take the extra steps to help improve their scores and teach them how important a good credit score would mean to them. Homeownership is better than renting. If you are renting, you are not building equity. Hopefully the goal is to become a homeowner, so we stay in contact with our clients and from time to time coach them to the point of owning their own home.

I purchased my first home for $48,000 and sold it ten years later for $150,000. I was able to put a nice down payment toward my next property and still have enough for the closing costs of a bigger home.

This is why I call it your biggest investment. We all blessed to live in America where we all have the opportunity to own real estate and build equity and wealth.

PROPERTY MANAGEMENT

L ike most real estate firms, our firm is a full-service property-management firm. Just like everything else, a good property manager can create wealth for you, while on the flip side, a not-so-good property manager could cause you to lose your pants.

Most big-box property-management companies have a whole division dedicated to property management. However, when hiring a property-management firm, ask if they are properly licensed and have the required insurances. Many states require all real estate companies to have a property-management license. A lot of real estate firms believe they don't need to be licensed in order to manage property. Real estate agents must also be licensed unless they are working under someone else's license.

Some real estate agents will tell you, "I could do the property management for you," but without the proper license and insurance, they could cause serious problems for you.

When you screen for a property manager, ask how many properties he or she is currently managing, if he or she is licensed, and if he or she has the proper insurance.

Make sure, when a property manager screens for a tenant on your behalf, the property manager runs a full credit report and background screening.

At our firm we do a seven-point credit and background check; plus we call the prior landlord to ensure quality tenants for our clients. We also allow the homeowner to interview the tenant in person or on phone.

Here is what we look for when screening potential tenants: We like candidates to have a credit score over six hundred, no evictions, and no criminal record. We also like to see their monthly income be three times over their monthly rent. For example, if they plan to rent a unit for $1,000 each month, we want to see an income of $3,000 each month with no exceptions. We also screen each occupant over eighteen and willcredit their income if they are employed. In our contract we also include a clause prohibiting overnight guests from staying more than fifteen days. Anyone staying over fifteen days may have intentions to live there full time. We ask to screen such individuals if we see any red flags and request that they be removed from the property if necessary. If their reports come back clean, we increase the rate by $10–$15 per month.

We drive by the property at least once over sixty days to insure the property is well maintained. You want to make sure that your property-management performs regular drive-by inspections. After all, it's your investment.

When you hire a property manager, make sure he or she is not subcontracting out the work. A lot of licensed companies acquire the contract from you and subcontract it out. This is seen more in multi-units; they hire someone with no experience and give them a title of assistance manager. You hire the property manager, and this property manager should be the one that manages your investment.

Evictions
You want to make sure that your property manager knows how to do evictions. We have a full team in place, including lawyers that specialize only in

evictions—process servers. The goal here is to kick the tenants out as quickly as possible.

Tenants not paying rent are tenants who are not paying you, and if you have to pay a mortgage this could place you in a financial predicament. This is the reason you need an expert managing your investment.

Hiring Options

You can hire a manager to manage the entire property to perform such services as hiring vendors, collecting rents, and doing repairs and receiving calls on your behalf. Another option is to hire a manager for partial management, performing any particular assignment you request. Every property is unique and requires different handling.

You want to make sure the property-management company that you hire answers its phones. This is the major problem I hear: "The property manager is unreachable, and the only time I am able to reach him or her is when it comes time to renew his or her contract."

If you do your own property management, always screen your tenants. I heard from one homeowner whose tenant only made one rent payment. Big problem. Always screen your tenants, and execute their leases. You will need a copy of the lease if you have to appear in court.

Yes, you could take on this venture on your own, but since it's an investment, I would recommend having a professional do the management.

Chapter Summary

MORTGAGES

I have been originating mortgages for quite a while, and, yes, I still find corruption in this industry. In 2007–2008 President Obama's government stepped in and revised the mortgage-lending guidelines due to all the corruption that was taking place. Now anyone originating mortgages must obtain a national license by attending a class and passing a national and state examination. This has slowed down the corruption quite a bit. It's very rare to run into a situation where corruption is taking place. I have been involved in the mortgage business for about six years and have only come across three instances of corruption during this time. Overall, it's very rare to be in a situation where the loan officer is committing fraud.

If you are buying a home, I would suggest you read this chapter twice. It can save you thousands of dollars from the closing cost to the life of the mortgage loan.

A lot of people really don't know that you can get retail and a wholesale interest rate. That is correct; you can get a wholesale rate that can usually save you 0.25–0.50 on your rate.

Retail rates usually come from your local neighborhood banks, credit unions, or national banks. The loan originator will not reveal this information to you. Most people just walk into their banks and apply for a mortgage because it seems safe and secure. Hey, I can't blame them. Since this industry had so much corruption, people are just tired of being ripped off.

They are many wholesale lenders out there that can offer you a good wholesale rate. To search just type in your browser "wholesale mortgage lenders," and you will be surprised by the amount of wholesale lenders you will find.

Everyone is concerned about points—the amount the lender charges to originate the loan. Many national banks claim they don't charge any points. Oh, really? Then who pays the loan officer? A loan officer does not work at the bank for free. The truth is most banks get it on the back end of the loan, which is called the yield spread premium (YSP). The YSP depends on the interest locked in for you. A bank could receive up to six points on the back end, and who ends up paying for it? This YSP is not disclosed on the closing statements because law states the lender doesn't have to reveal the YSP.

If you are not being charged any points up front, chances are that you are not getting the best interest rate. Ask a lot of questions. This will lead to getting the best rate for your loan.

Here's another very important point: I walk into one those local national banks, and right in front, there is a sign with rates displayed on it. I say to myself, wow, they're offering good rates, and then I look at the annual percentage rate of charge (APR).

Here is what is displayed: thirty years fixed at 3.25 percent, but in small print, the APR is 4.75 percent. The APR is what you are actually paying for the loan. The APR is all the junk fees the lender could stick inside your loan; these include underwriting fees, processing fees, application fees, points orgination fees, and whatever else can be added in.

Most people would only pay attention to the advertised rate of 3.25 percent without realizing that they will be actually be paying 4.75 percent, the true rate. I once went to purchase a car, and the finance guy told me the rate would be 2 percent. I asked him what the APR would be. He hesitated and replied that the APR would be 3.99 percent. I told him that

I could get a better loan than what he offered. He immediately reduced all those junk fees, making my APR 2.5 percent.

Let's get back to the points. Sometimes it's better to pay points up front. This will reduce your APR. If the lender's compensation rate is 2 percent (points), this may be better for you getting a better rate.

Here is an example. Let's say you are trying to get the lowest possible rate, and you are working with a lender with a 2 percent compensation rate. Your options would be as follows:

3.25 percent (100 par)
3.5 percent (101)
3.75 percent (102)
4 percent (103)

The best rate for you without going out of pocket to buy the rate would be 3.75 percent. This includes any adjustments for the credit score, property type, location of the property, and so forth.

You may be asking yourself why you couldn't get the 3.25 percent rate. Remember the lender's compensation rate is 2 percent. That means if your loan amount is $100,000, you would have to pay out of your pocket $2,000 for this rate, increasing your closing cost.

Now let's take a look at one of those major banks' compensations. They will tell you that they don't charge any points, and here's the reason why. Their options would be as follows:

    3.25 percent (100 par)
    3.5 percent (101)
    3.75 percent (102)
    4.00 percent (103)
    4.12 percent (104)
    4.25 percent (105)
    4.5 percent (106)

Take a guess which rate you will end up getting? Depending on the retail bank's parameters, you will be pitched 4–4.5 percent. Many banks want to make a YSP of six points.

Sometimes it's better to pay a few points up front. Would you rather have a rate of 3.75 percent compared to 4 percent? One-fourth percent could save you thousands of dollars over the life of a mortgage loan.

Credit
Credit is very important. We usually rapidly rescore most of our clients' FICO scores to 640 or above. Six hundred forty is the magic number for lenders. It's easier to underwrite, and the client will be able to get a better interest rate. Do you think that someone

with a FICO score of 500 should be able to get the same rate as someone with a FICO score of 700?

Do you need to increase your credit score by five to sixty points? Here's an insider secret I will reveal to you. Have you ever noticed on your credit report, usually on the top of the page, where it shows all those addresses you lived for the previous fifteen years? Removing those addresses from your report will increase your score by five to sixty points. When I did this, I couldn't believe it.

Lenders can make adjustments to your credit score. I have seen up to two points added for scores below 640. This means that a person with a score of 600 would most likely receive a much higher rate -. A lot of people are unaware of this and simply think they qualify for mortgage loan. That may be true, but their rate wouldn't be the best.

If you are shopping for a mortgage loan, do yourself a favor and get your score over 640. It will be less of a headache for you and save you thousands of dollars over the lifetime of the loan.

Shopping Around
Now you have information about some basics of mortgages, and you are all geared up to confront a lender. But where should you go next? Should you go to a lender, bank, or mortgage broker?

You've already learned that you need to go to a wholesale lender, so what about a mortgage broker?

If you are going to use a broker, make sure the broker is a wholesaler. Mortgage brokers are very good because they work with multiple lenders that offer different products and prices. All mortgage brokers have to do is plug your information into their systems, and within minutes the software will pick the very best product for you. Some brokers may work with fifty to seventy-five lenders. This may be a good place to start.

Direct wholesale lenders are very similar to mortgage brokers. The difference is that they fund the loan in their own business name. Direct lenders work with many different investors that purchase their loans directly from them. Many direct lenders work with thirty to forty investors just like a mortgage broker.

Debt-to-Income Ratio

Here's another subject that you must be aware of. Debt-to-income ratio (DTI) is very important in qualifying for a home loan. Here's how it works in a nutshell. Take your gross income, and add up your monthly obligation, including your mortgage or the total mortgage payment of the property you are buying. Remember to add principle, interest, taxes, and insurance.

Let's say your gross monthly income is $8,000 and your total debt is $3,500: 3,500/8,000 = 44 percent.

To qualify for a conventional loan, your DTI must be less than 50 percent. If you are applying for a FHA loan, your DTI must be less than 55 percent. This is the reason most people would apply for a FHA loan. It's much easier.

Chapter Summary

Most lending professionals are on the level and will do their very best to get you the loan. There is not a lot of corruption nowadays, and these professionals are always under the gun to meet the lenders guidelines and deadlines. For the most part, the government and not lenders are in control. . Lenders are in business to originate loans, not to fund and hold the loans for a long period. If they approved a loan and closed on it and the secondary market wouldn't buy the loan from the lender, that lender would have to keep the loan, costing them several thousands of dollars.

If you are planning to purchase a home, your first step is to get preapproval for a loan. Most Realtors will not show you any properties until they know you qualify for a loan. I knew of an agent who showed a client eighteen homes to purchase, without a pre-approval..

If you are selling a property, make sure that you are working with a Realtor who understands mortgages and qualifications to obtain a loan. If the Realtor tells you to accept an offer without knowing if the buyer actually qualifies for a home loan, you could be tied into a contract for months. I've heard stories of property been tied up for five months, and the buyer couldn't get the loan. The seller wasn't pleased. Do yourself a favor. If you are selling, work with an expert. Don't work with anyone who doesn't have a clue. Remember that this is a business transaction on your biggest investment.

If you would like to receive some additional information on credit or mortgages, please reach out to us via e-mail, and we will respond.

TITLE COMPANIES

In most states all parties involved in a real estate transaction have the right to choose a closing agent to represent their side of the transaction. A lot of buyers and sellers are unaware of this. This knowledge could save you hundreds of dollars in closing costs.

Every item on the closing disclosure is negotiable expect for government recording fees, taxes, and mortgage and deed stamps. The remaining items are set prices from the title company such as title-service fees. I have seen these fees ranging from $3,200 to as low as $300 and notary fees from $60 to $300.

When our firm is involved in a transaction and we are not using one of our preferred title companies, we always ask for the title company's fee sheet before we make any type of commitment. If you are a buyer or a seller, make sure that your real estate agent has some experience dealing with title companies and understands closing fees. Most big-box real estate companies have their own title company, require their agents to use their firm's title company, and offer them some sort of incentive for directing their clients to use it. Remember that if a title company is charging you $1,200 for title services, they are charging the other side of the transaction the same $1,200 for title services. That amounts to $2,400 just for title services. Whatever they charge you, they are most likely charging the other side the same. A title company could make as much as $3,000–$10,000 for a real estate closing, so negotiate, negotiate, negotiate!

I once had a transaction a cash buyer and a seller that owned the property free and clear. I asked the title company why there was a wiring fee of $80, especially when no money was being wired. I was told that it was a standard fee. Actually, a title company can't charge you for a service that isn't being used. This is Real Estate Settlement Procedure Act (RESPA) violation and could have been reported to the CFPB.

Established in 1975, RESP, also called Regulation X, is a federal law to protect consumers. This law protects consumers from title companies with cost of real estate settlement processes, kickbacks, and escrow bank accounts.

When you make your good faith or earnest money deposit into a title company's bank account, the holder of that account must send you an escrow letter. Also, I always ask if the account bears interest. If it's an interest-bearing account, the interest should be credited back to the client with the deposit. This information should also be disclosed up front to all parties. A lot companies are unwilling to share this information, but it's a requirement. Most of these title companies carry over a million dollars of balance in their escrow account, making them additional income from just the interest. Lawyer-based title companies are more likely to have interest-bearing accounts than other types of title companies because holding interest-bearing accounts is heavily regulated.

In the past there was a lot of corruption associated with title companies. I have heard of stories about title companies not paying off or sending the collected money to pay off mortgages from the sale. Fraudulent companies were set up to do about ten closings and take off with the funds to pay off the mortgages and pay the title insurance premium. I have been a witness where we represented a seller that had to sell his property after two years of ownership and requested a copy of the title policy only to find out that the title company never paid for the policy; instead, the title company had pocketed the money.

Title Policy

I am a big believer that the buyer should purchase the owner's title policy. Do you really want the seller to pick and pay for an insurance policy on your behalf? This is like having a complete stranger buying cut-rate health insurance on your behalf. If you are buying, you want to make sure you get the best owner title policy. The owner title protects homeowners from others making a claim on their property. That's correct. I have heard of scams when the home was sold, and some distant relative made a claim that the property was legally theirs. Without a proper owner policy, you may be forced to surrender your property.

Lawyer-Based Title Companies versus Non-Attorney-Based Title Companies

Let start first with a lawyer-based title company. I know most buyers and sellers may think that it's always better to use a lawyer to close a real estate transaction. The answer is yes and no. In my opinion it would be better to use an attorney to handle your real estate transaction, but here are the facts: Most attorneys don't prepare the closing documents.

They use an office clerk or a third-party processor to prepare the closing documents. They're simply too busy to figure out perorations, recording fees, and so forth. Most importantly, they are more expensive than a non-attorney-based title company. They know the law and know what they can legally charge for. If a transaction becomes complicated between parties, it's best to have an attorney. For the most part, finding a lawyer-based title company with reasonable fees may be the best solution for you. But always request a fee sheet beforehand, and keep in mind, as stated before, they are more expensive than non-attorney-based closing agents.

Our company uses a non-attorney-based title company about 95 percent of the time. These types of closing agents usually prepare their own documents and process them faster. The most important reason we use them is because they are cheaper and can always get the clients the very best rates on title policies. In reality they are simply insurance agents and must hold a state-issued insurance-agent license. They work with major title-policy companies and have a better relationship with the underwriters within these companies. They are also required to take continuing education classes every year and are monitored more closely than a lawyer-based title company. Plus, you can always reach the person assigned to your file, which is very important to me and my clients.

Chapter Summary

Work with a real estate agent who understands the closing process and can interrupt closing documents. An expert real agent could save you hundreds of dollars in closing costs. . If a title company won't send you a fee sheet or states they don't have a fee sheet, move on to the next title company. The reason for them not having a fee sheet is to charge you as much as possible. Most buyers and sellers will only participate in a real estate transaction every seven to ten years or longer. Many consumers assume that the real estate agent is the expert; this may not be the case. Many big-box real estate firms own their own title company, and the broker may demand using his or her company by giving out incentives. This is a gray area. Remember RESP? Section 8 of RESP contains regulations for kickbacks.

I recommend working with an expert agent. This is a must. With the proper agent guiding you, you can save hundreds of dollars and save yourself from many headaches.

Most agents will just assign everything over to a title company thinking their job is done without even checking the fees or processing their own closing documents.

It's really the agent's responsibility to take care of the clients in every aspect of a real estate transaction.

If you are doing this on your own, I advise you to do your due diligence.

Our firm likes using small title companies. Whether they are a lawyer based or not, we receive more personal and caring attention from small companies. Having a smooth transaction is what it's all about. There is already enough stress involved when you are buying and selling real estate.

SELLING A HOME

Selling a property is not the same as selling a car—it's far from it. If you are selling a home, you have to understand that you have to enter into a legally binding contract. This is the major difference between selling a car and selling a property. Anyone can sell a car. All you have to do is to take a few pictures of the car and list it on one of those online car-selling sites. Once you sell it, all you have to do is sign over the title, or if you still owe money on your car, pay off your car note and then send the car's title to the buyer's lender.

When I first started investing in real estate, I thought I could sell a house myself. I learned the hard way that there are far too many moving parts in selling real estate. If you are unfamiliar with real estate contracts, title companies, appraisals, mortgages, and lender's guidelines, I highly recommend hiring an expert. One hundred percent of my real estate investment transactions involved a real estate agent. That's the reason I became a real estate agent. If you have an expert buyer's agent, he or she will sniff out your inexperience and take full advantage of the situation. I lost thousands of dollars simply because I didn't know this important fact.

Face it. If you don't sell real estate as a profession, there's a good chance you will lose money on your transaction. It may be cheaper in the long run to hire a Realtor.

Real estate is a business. Since it involves one of your biggest investments, get an expert. This cannot be stressed enough.

The main reason I set off to sell my own properties was to save money. But I still needed expert advice. I lost money on repairs that I didn't have to attend to, on closing costs I didn't need to have paid, and by unnecessarily lowering the sale price of the property. After the closing, I added up the numbers to find that I didn't make the amount of money I'd anticipated.

Ninety-five percent of properties of "For Sale by Owner" sellers will eventually be listed with a real estate agent. This happens after these owners experience the magnitude of what it takes to sell real estate. Typically, this happens when "For Sale by Owner" sellers list their properties with some flat-rate service and they soon realize that the only calls they're receiving are from real estate agents. Real estate agents are aware that 95 percent of "For Sale by Owner" sellers will list their property with a real estate agent.

Once you decided that it's best for you to go ahead and list with a Realtor, here are the things you need to know:

1) Calculate how much money you anticipate making on the sale of the property. Take your last mortgage statement, and find the balance you owe. Figure out the amount of commission that must be paid out. Have a realistic listing price and a floor price. Calculate an estimated closing cost. A good way to estimate your closing cost is to multiply 2–3 percent of the selling price.

2) Commission rates are negotiable. If agents explain to you that they are unable to make any adjustments to the commission rates, keep looking. Important point: selling real estate is hard work, and you need to be reasonable. By this I mean that if your property is located in a hot market area, there's a good

chance you could reduce the commission rate. If you own a high-end property—let's say over $500,000—there's a good chance that you could reduce the commission rate. If you have a property that needs major work or needs to be modernized, there's a good chance the commission rate will not be reduced. If your property is located in a heavy crime area, there's a good chance that the commission rate won't be reduced. You get the idea. So you need to be reasonable and somewhat flexible.

Every situation is different just like every property is unique. I once had a client that needed to sell but didn't have enough equity (money) to move and relocate to another state. We structured the transaction to fit the client's needs by agreeing on a flat-fee rate for selling and paying the buyer's agent at 2 percent. The client was extremely happy not because she was able to reach her financial goals but because the home was sold within forty-five days.

You want to make sure that your real estate agent can be flexible on his or her commission rates; this can save you thousands of dollars. It drives me crazy to see sellers get taken advantage of because they didn't know and didn't take the time to research their options. I have seen properties selling for much less than their neighbors and their owners paying more commissions. Take a look at this actual example:

House A: Four bedrooms, three bathrooms, 1,500 square feet selling for $250,000 with a commission rate of 4 percent.

House B: Three bedrooms, two bathrooms, 1,500 square feet selling for $200,000 with a commission rate of 6 percent.

Both houses are located next to each other. Let's find out which seller paid more in commission.

House A is selling for $250,000 and paying a 4 percent commission of $10,000.

House B is selling for $200,000 and paying 6 percent commission of $12,000.

Although House B is selling for less and is inferior to House A, its seller ended up paying more than House A's seller. The difference is $2,000. Why? Is the real agent doing more marketing or other extra work? The answer, of course, is no. It simply means that the seller of House A negotiated a much better commission deal on his or her behalf.

If your agent finds a buyer, take it a step further by agreeing on another reduction on the commission. I often offer a reduction in the commission to my clients if I locate a buyer. Why? Because agents will often set on a property if they think that property is hot and could easily be sold. They will not set any appointments with any other agent and will wait until they can find a buyer in order to keep a bigger commission split. If you agree on a commission of 6 percent with your agent, they would have to share half, or 3 percent, but if they find the buyer they will keep the entire 6 percent. This is called a pocket listing. In order to prevent making this kind of agreement, if the agent finds a buyer, the commissions need to be reduced. If you are selling your property to buy another in the same market area, have the agent reduce his or her share of the commission from the sale of your home, and the agent will make another commission when you purchase another property.

Flat-Rate Services

Flat-rate services are exactly what they sound like— services that cost flat rates. Remember, as I stated earlier, I use flat-rate MLS listing services to sell my properties. With this type of service, all you get is your property listed on the MLS, which makes the inexperienced seller without the help of an expert an easy target. By not having anybody representing you, there's a good chance that you will be taken for some money. Lack of experience and knowledge can place you into some jeopardy. If you are using a flat rate to save on commission now that you know you can negotiate on the commission, you understand the importance of having an expert guiding you all the way to the closing table. Plus with all the scams that are currently going on, you want to know who is entering your home. Having the proper expert guiding you means cutting the risk of doing business and losing your hard-earned equity.

Discount Brokerage Firms

When using discounted real estate brokerage firms, make sure that the agent you trust puts everything in writing. I have heard stories where the seller expects to pay only a 1 percent commission to one of these discounted brokerage firms only to find out about additional fees for listing services, administration fees, compliance fees, and you name it. The fees will add on. Get the listing agreement in writing before placing your name on a contract. No, you don't have to get an attorney. Most real estate contracts are written by lawyers and approved by the National Realtor Board. Also, only have your listing agreement extend for ninety days, if the agent is not producing it will allow a way out in a reasonable time. This is what we do in our firm. All listing agreements are valid for ninety days. It's a two-way street. Some agents may not be compatible with the seller, and of course the seller may think that the agent isn't producing. My belief is that if you are unable to get buyers into your property and under a contract in ninety days, there's no effort being made.

Basics of the Sale

The first chapter on real estate agents should give you the basics to find an expert real estate agent to help coach you all the way to the closing table. Don't forget to ask questions. This is the only way to pinpoint the right match for you and give the agent the feeling that you have some good knowledge about real estate transactions.

Here are some dos and don'ts:

- Hire a professional photographer. Ninety-nine percent of buyers are searching the Internet for homes. Professional photos of a home attract more buyers to the home. A video can be an added bonus. Putting it on YouTube adds an even bigger plus. All of our agents add a YouTube video to their listings.
- Keep your property clean. Don't leave dirty dishes around in the kitchen.
- Be prepared to leave your property while it's being shown. Most buyers want to feel at ease when looking at a property. They don't want to feel rushed, and your being there tends to

make them feel rushed. If you have pets, take them along with you. A lot of people don't like pets.

- Keep up on your landscaping, remove trash around your home, and if you have a pool, make sure it's running and it's clean.

- No need to paint the property. Most home-buyers will paint the home once they move in. Everyone is different. The color you pick may not be liked by others.

- Be reasonable about your sale price. You don't want to be priced too high. You won't get any potential buyers. If an agent tells you to list for $20,000–$30,000 more than what the property is worth, your home will sit on the market for a long time. When buyers are searching and come across your listing after it has been sitting there for eight months, they will pass it by, thinking that there must be some issues with the home. In my opinion it's never a good idea to list a property higher than fair market value only to have to lower the price. The objective is to sell it. Even if at first it seems that you can sell it for more, you will still have to deal with the appraisal, meaning you may still have to match the ap-praisal price. You want to list your property for a reasonable price. Having your agent do a competitive market analysis will be a go-to tool to select your listing price. You want to be just below the highest listing in your area. This is key.

Upgrades don't really increase your home's value. If you're considering upgrading all your appliances, thinking it's going to bring you an extra $10,000 or adding upgraded flooring, remember what the appraiser is looking for in home value—the fair market value that a person would pay. Let's say that you and your neighbors have identical homes, but you added new appliances and upgraded the flooring, and you're thinking that your home is worth $20,000 more than your neighbors. The answer is no; the appraisal will look at all the homes that had been sold in your area that are similar to yours and come up with the fair market value of your home. Some appraisers will give some credit to upgrades but never par credit.

A pool will add an additional $5,000–$10,000 to the value of your home. If you think that if you paid $50,000 for your pool, it should instantly add $50,000 to your home value, you would be wrong. It depends on the appraiser giving you credit, and I can guarantee you that it wouldn't be at face value.

Place air fresheners around your home. People like to walk in a home and smell a nice soft scent of flowers.

Here is another tip: Kitchens and bathrooms sell homes, so keep those areas spotless. I sold a home because the husband loved the cleanliness of an electric range. I sold another home because the wife loved the landscaping. It really doesn't take too much. Just keep it clean, don't paint unless it's needed, and don't add any upgrades.

Chapter Summary
You could do it on your own, but your objective is to make as much as possible from your investment. Having an expert guiding you and leading you is the best plan. Of course, if you are selling real estate professionally, you should be able to handle it on your own. But if this is your first or second time out selling a property, please seek expert advice.

If you are still thinking that you could be saving money by doing it on your own, ask yourself some basic questions:

- Are you sure you have the property listed at a reasonable price? Is the price too low? Do you know your market value? Having an expert do a market analysis will give a threshold on your listing price.
- Are you prepared to invite complete strangers into your home with all the scams taking

place? Do you really want to place this type of risk on your family?

- How familiar are you with title-company charges? Having an expert could save you hundreds of dollars. I have lost a lot of money before I understood this subject. I once paid $1,700 for title services. Why? I didn't know that I could negotiate with the title company. Nobody told me that was possible.

- Are you sure that the buyer is really qualified to buy your property? Having an expert could eliminate the risk of having your property tied up for months.

- Do you have an open permit? I come across this issue often, especially with older homes. Usually the homeowners think the contractors have closed out the permit, but sometimes they haven't. An open permit could delay your closing by weeks or even months; however, an expert Realtor could clear up an open permit in time for your closing.

I am not a believer in staging a home. This means fooling people, and most buyers already have their own furniture. If you are selling a high-end property, this might be a good idea, but a good professional cleaning before the home goes onto the market will be just fine. Sometimes I will hire a professional interior decorator to guide us on rearranging the home decor. This is less expensive and effective.

Figure out on what you really need to net from the sale of the property, and the rest of the items will fall into place.

Negotiate your commission fees, but you need to be reasonable. It's a lot of work and involves things that you may not be familiar with. All the behind-the-scenes issues can cause you a lot of trouble. Most agents are trained to resolve most of these issues.

But you first must acknowledge what you need to net from the sale of the property. This is a key factor. Don't reveal your floor price to anyone. If asked, quote them a few thousand over your floor price.

Interview multiple real estate agents to determine which one will be the best match for you. Once you narrow your selection and you decided on your agent of choice, only sign a ninety-day listing agreement. A good agent can save you a lot of money and headaches compared to doing it yourself.

An expert real estate agent can also help you hire a reparative moving company and a professional cleaning service. On day of or day before your closing date, there are a lot of things that must be done. I recommend using the real estate agent to make these types of arrangements. You don't need all the added stress.

Your real estate agent can also help you with post-closing issues like getting back your escrow deposit or issues with the property that happen often.

Real estate is a business and must be treated as such. After all, it involves one of your biggest investments, so you require an expert to guide you to the finish line.

BUYERS

If you are planning to purchase a home, I will urge you to reread the chapter on mortgages. By far this is the first step you would need to accomplish before even thinking of buying a home. If you are paying cash for your home, you have an upper hand. If you plan to finance it, you would need to find out how much you will qualify for. You would also need to understand the terms of your preapproval. For instance, if the lender issues you a preapproval letter for $300,000, you would need to know the parameters of his or her calculations. Every home is unique. Every home has a different value as far as property taxes and the amount of insurance required. Most lenders will simply guess on the taxes and insurance and issue a preapproval letter to just to get your business.

This could be a major problem if you make a good faith deposit on a home and you don't qualify for the loan. So ask the lender the amount of taxes and insurance the lender used to make the calculations.

Here's an example: Let's say you received a preapproval for $300,000 and the lender based the calculations for property taxes at $1,800 per year and the insurance at $600 per year. You find a home for $300,000 and place an offer plus a good faith deposit of $10,000, and your offer is accepted. However, the taxes on the property that you are buying are $7,000 per year, the insurance is $4,000 per year, and the homeowner association (HOA) dues are $250 per month. Because the property you are buying has much higher taxes, HOA dues, and the insurance cost, this will increase your debt-to-income ratios. If you finance a conventional loan, your maximum debt-to-income ratio is 50 percent. If you go through an FHA loan, the maximum debt-to-income ratio is 55 percent.

You want to make sure you know the parameters of the preapproval and stay within those parameters. If not, you could find yourself with some problems and expenses, such as paying for an appraisal and a home inspection and even losing your good faith deposit. We have seen it all when clients come to us to rescue their transaction after finding out they actually qualify for a much lower amount than they expected. In Florida, if there is any dispute over the good faith deposit, it must go to a parliament proceeding.

So the first step is to get that preapproval letter and ask questions about the calculation on the taxes, insurance, and any type of monthly dues. Make sure you have full confidence and trust with the lender or loan officer. If for any reason you are on the fence, move on to another lender. Trust yourself. Ask around to make sure that the lender is up to par.

Working with a Real Estate Agent

Now that you are ready to start shopping for a home, do you do so on your own or hire a real estate agent? Ninety-five percent of buyers will use a real estate agent to shop for a home. It's free to hire a real estate agent; however, we have noticed a trend across the country that real estate agents are now making buyers sign an agreement and pay a retainer fee. Being a real estate agent is the only profession that you work for free before you get paid. When we hire a lawyer, contractor, accountant, or just about any professional, we have to pay a deposit or retainer. This is the very reason the industry is changing. To be honest, I would charge a retainer fee if I believed the client was using me to kick the tires and not serious about doing any transaction. It takes a real estate agent a lot of research and time to set up appointments, so I am a strong supporter of retainer fees.

Now that you've found your real estate agent, I would highly recommend first meeting with the agent and providing him or her with your wish list. Included on this list should be the size, style, and location of the home you're looking for and your budget—the most important item on this list. Have the agent show you what is available to your liking. This way both you and your agent can be on the same page. Once your agent has an understanding of what you are looking for, the agent should enter your information into his or her system so you can receive a daily inventory of properties right in your e-mail's inbox.

I would also recommend visiting these properties during the week, not on the weekend. Why? Most people are working Monday through Friday, 9:00 a.m. to 5:00 p.m., and shopping for homes on the weekend. If you can look at properties on weekdays, you will be ahead of the game because you will be first to see the properties before the weekend crowd.

I always make arrangements with my clients to look for property during the work week around 3:00–6:00 p.m. so we can have a chance to speak to the homeowner, look at the rush hour traffic, and get a better feel of the neighborhood when people are coming home. I will also inform our clients to go back around 8:00–9:00 p.m. just to make sure that the area is suitable and safe.

You don't want to buy a home and find out that your neighbors are throwing nightly parties or have twenty cars parked in front of their homes. Buying a home is an investment into your future, and you want to make sure that you have found that perfect home for you and your family.

Placing alerts on different websites for properties that are just coming onto the market can help you find more listings. This is a great way to be the first to visit a home and place an offer. Your agent is most likely working with other clients and will need your help as well to locate properties. This is a team effort, and communication channels must be open in order to accomplish your goals.

Finally you found a home and placed an offer, and the contract is executed. Congratulations. But hold up, grasshopper, and remember there are many moving parts in a real estate transaction. This is when your real estate expert blossoms. I always have my clients hire their own home inspector. I furnish a list so they can call and interview the inspector. Not all home inspectors are equal. The ones we have listed have been vetted. If the clients don't like any of our recommended vendors, I will have them do their own research for a home inspector. Most home inspectors will find issues with the property. It could be something as simple as having the air condition unit serviced or something more complex like the roof needing to be replaced. Let's say the home inspector tells you that the roof needs to be replaced. Do you back away or renegotiate your offer? This will depend on you. Usually a roof replacement will run you between $7,000 and $25,000. Would the seller be willing to reduce the price by $25,000, or do you have $25,000 to pay to replace the roof? Most lenders will not approve the loan if there are any serious damages to the home. They will reject the collateral due to the necessity for major repairs.

If your inspection report comes back with just simple minor repairs, and you feel confident enough to move forward, your next huddle will be the appraisal. This could jeopardize your transaction. Let's say you are buying the home for $300,000 and the appraisal report comes back as a fair market value of $230,000. Yes, this could stop you from moving forward, and most sellers will not come down more than $2,000–$10,000 on their sale price.

Make sure that your real estate agent does a comparison market analysis before submitting any offer and also includes an appraisal contingency with the offer. This alone can save you a lot of grief. Remember a real estate contract is a legal contract, and if there is any dispute you may end up in a courtroom.

If the home inspection report and the appraisal come in positive, congratulations! But again, hold up grasshopper, we still have to deal with title and lien searches. Most older homes may have open permits that haven't been closed or satisfied with the county where the property is located. If your title agent comes across any open permits or open liens, your real estate agent will help you and the seller clear them up before the contract date. If there are any code violations, such as an illegal addition, the lender will not approve the loan until the structure is revised or completely knocked down.

As you can see, there are a lot of moving parts involved in a real estate transaction. This is the reason you need to work with an expert real estate agent. An expert Realtor can guide you from financing all the way to the closing table.

SUMMARY

Get approved for a loan first, and know all the parameters about your approval. A lot of buyers are not aware of the extra steps involved in the approval process. Having a preapproval letter for $300,000 doesn't mean you can buy any home for $300,000. Look at the property taxes, hazard insurance cost, and any homeowner monthly dues. Don't waste your time without knowing these parameters.

Hire a real estate agent. Most people have friends or relatives who are agents, but these people may not be the best match for you. Interview multiple agents. You know which one will be a better fit for you. It's OK if they ask for a retainer or contract between you and the agent. Most retainer fees are credited back to you once you close on a property. Make sure your agent comprehends the type, style, and location of the property that you are shopping for. If an agent doesn't seem to be on the same page as you and shows you properties outside your limits, move on to another agent.

You can use a full-time, part-time, seasoned, or newcomer agent; it's all about you having confidence in your real estate agent. This is a pretty big investment on your behalf, and you don't want someone handling your transaction that seems clueless.

Home Inspection
Interview multiple state certified, licensed home inspectors. If a home inspector is not licensed, run. I have seen home inspectors finish an entire inspection on a home with four bedrooms, two bathrooms, and a two-car garage within forty-five minutes. Nobody can do a home inspection in an hour, even if it's on a five-hundred-square-foot condo. An average, medium-size home should take four to six hours. The typical cost for a home inspection is $350–$800, which, of course, depends on the size of the home.

Once your contract has been fully executed, start looking for a home inspector. Most agents do not recommend just any home inspector due to liability, but many provide you with a list of home inspectors.

Ultimately it's up to you—the buyer—to hire your home inspector.

I like to do the home inspection before the lender orders the appraisal because it will rule out any major repairs that need to be made. If repairs need to be made, the seller reduces the sale price or makes the necessary repairs before the closing date. Ask the seller the age of the roof. If it's older than ten years, it may be time to replace it. If the seller tells you the roof is twenty years old, and there has never been a problem with it, be warned. An old roof is like driving around on a worn tire: at some point that tire will become flat. Before we enter into a contract, we usually find out the age of the roof because repairing a roof can be the most expensive work performed on a home.

A home inspection is extremely important and not to be taken for granted. Imagine moving into your dream home and finding out that the electrical panel is failing and blowing a fuse every ten minutes, the air condition unit is not blowing cool air, the washer and dryer are not working, bathrooms are backing up, or worse yet the roof is leaking water after a light rain. You get the point. The inspection is a very important component in a real estate transaction, so take your time. No need to rush. Hire a well-qualified home inspector.

Appraisal

You—the buyer—can't pick the appraiser. The lender hires an appraisal management company to perform the appraisal. The appraisal is basically an opinion from the appraiser on what the fair market value of the property is and what buyers would likely purchase the property for. You don't want to pay more for something than it's actually worth—that's human nature. The appraiser contacts the seller and the seller's real estate agent to make arrangements to visit the property. You, as the buyer, have limited involvement in the appraisal process, and most appraisers do not communicate directly with the real estate agents. It may take up to two weeks to get the appraisal report. The report has to go through a quality-control process and be reviewed by two or more appraisers. This is to prevent any type of fraud and to protect the consumers.

If your real estate agent performs a comparable market analysis before submitting the offer, the numbers shouldn't be that far off. For added protection, always have your agent submit an appraisal contingency with your offer—this is a must. This will allow you to walk away from the contract in case the appraisal comes back short and let you negotiate with the seller. It's one of the most powerful documents you have on your side as a buyer. On most FHA contracts, the FHA addendum includes an appraisal clause in it, but I like to include the appraisal contingency regardless.

Relax. The appraisal should come in on point. Your agent will have shown you properties similar to the one you are purchasing that sold within the last six months, so you can be confident that the numbers should be on point or very close. Most sellers will negotiate or come down to the appraisal value. This is the reason we use an appraisal contingency.

Title Companies

If you are the buyer, you must be the one that picks the closing agent to work on your behalf. Since you have to purchase an owner title policy, who better to pick the insurance agent than you? You don't want the seller buying insurance on your behalf. It's your policy, so pick your own closing agent. Most people are unaware that most title companies are just simply insurance agents. They have to get a state-issued insurance license. All the other stuff like lien searches, estoppels, and recordings are contracted out to a third party. The closing agent's main function is to just issue a title policy.

You should always ask for a fee sheet before deciding on a title company. Every company's charges are different. We have seen title-service fees ranging from $350 to $3,200. A reasonable fee for title services should average around $500–$750.

Most of the fees on a closing disclosure are negotiable except for the governmental recording and taxes, so your agent can recommend a title agent to perform your closing.

CONCLUSION

I hope this brief guide on buying a home is helpful and informs you where to do a little more research as you pursue your goal. Buying a home is a huge step for you and your family. It is an investment toward your future. Just think of every monthly payment going back into your pocket by building equity. If you purchase a home for $300,000, do you think that this home will be worth $300,000 in ten years? Your home will appreciate over the years, so the value of your $300,000 will be worth more in ten years. This is what got me involved in real estate. It's my opinion that this is the very best investment an average person can make.

The tax benefits are useful too, allowing you to write off the interest each and every year until your home is paid in full.

Most real estate agents enjoy working with buyers. For the most part, real estate agents work hard to provide the best results for buyers. Realtors have more and more tools to assist a buyer than a seller or an investor. Assisting you—the buyer—is the reason the National Association of Realtors set up one of the most popular websites: Realtor.com.

Real Estate Investing
YES, YES, YES, I am guilty! I have purchase thousands of dollars on how to get rich on buying and flipping real estate. The true answer is yes you could make a lot of money buying and selling properties, however you would need money to be successful. One year I flipped 8 properties it may not seem like whole lot to most, but for me it was accomplished goal.

My first property I purchase was a pre-foreclosure, I purchase a list of people that were greater than 90 days behind their mortgage payments. You could buy this list on-line there are multiple companies that could provide this list for you. I got smarter and purchased this list directly from the one of credit bureau. Well I mail out a modest amount of post cards, and usually received 3 -4 calls from the mailings

Well this poor elderly family found them- self in a big pickle the husband well let just say he had some habits. They were almost a year late on their mortgage payments, so I listen to them and come to find out they had no family and even worse no money. My question where are you planning to move to?

I wasn't a real estate agent as of yet, this my very first deal - a real rookie! Now, we made a agreement that they will give back $3000 to the homeowners, just enough to move somewhere close by. Now I have to deal with the big bad monster the lender.

This was in the early 90's no internet just fax was the very latest technology at that time. I wrote a nice letter to the lender (Key Bank in Cleveland) I received a call a week later from nice lady, and she stated that we could probably do a short sale. Short sale what is the hell is that- I asked her. She went on and explain if I could get the current homeowners financial statements it may be a good chance for me to purchase the property at a discount, so I did. A week or two went by, and I received another call from this nice lady asking me if I could close by next week Friday - we could close, and sell or discount the note for me for $40,000.00.

What do you think I say? Ah yes! So, I give the $3000 to the family, help them move rehab the property and 4 months later sold it for $77,000.00 oh boy I was hook!

So now I am real estate investor at least I think I am. Because I am working a full-time job sometimes

50 -55 hours per week I really didn't have the time to manage contractors. Anyway, I bought another pre-foreclosure property but this time I received what is called a hard money loan. It really what it says - it is hard money. Where I paid 5% upfront and 12% interest! I told myself what a great way to make money without dealing with these contractors and all the other problems dealing with rehabbing. I went ahead with the transaction bought the property for a $100,000 sold it after 4.5 months for $140,000.00 not bad right? Really think about it I had to close on this property twice meaning double closing cost plus the cost for rehab, and the cost for the loan. Yep, I made a few dollars. But I always remember what a great way to make money in real estate by lending your money, you just set back collect the upfront fees and monthly interest , if I could do this I don't have to worry about the contractors and spending money for the rehab and all those closing cost. No sweat equity, just collect what is call passive income - I liked this idea. So, research the hike out of this and found out that they are people that are doing passive investments. I got hook up with a company in Las Vegas that would allow me to invest $10,000.00 in what is call fractionalized mortgages. I did, I collected money every month 12% - up to 17% income coming in each and every month and the end I still get back my $10,000.00. Wow I must have done this

for about five years. Until one day out of the blue I received a called from the account Rep. She asked me if I would be interesting in buying a non-performing mortgage note, & I asked what is this? She explained that the homeowner is delinquent and the lender is considering selling this note at a heavy discount. It was discounted 30 cents on the dollar. I told her that she must be crazy why would I buy a non performing mortgage and not receive any monthly payments like what I have became accustom to receiving cash flow each and every month.

A few days went by, just like anything else I research all about non-performing notes, but I couldn't find any information. Anyway, I called her back and I ask how can I make any money from this investment? She went on and explained that that I could offer the homeowner a loan modification, short sale, cash for keys and last foreclose on them. And then I ask her how much I could buy this note for & to my surprise it was heavily discounted. I went the next day wire her the money, and the next day received a Fedex package with all these documents. I didn't know what I was looking at. I called my attorney and explain to him what I just purchased and he called me crazy! I meet up with him and told him what the Rep had told me what we could offer the homeowner. My attorney called me about 2 weeks later and stated that the homeowner is interesting on doing a loan modification and agreed to pay up-front fee of $15,000 if we could offer a low fixed rate for 30 years - yah baby. We did, we modified it drew up a nice mortgage and now collecting monthly payments. Now I am getting mortgage payment I am the bank! After a year, I received a call from a servicing company asking me if I am willing to sell my note to them- and reply why? They person stated I could collect a lump sum of money right away, so I did the math and call him back a few days later to wrap up this deal.

My friends I made a killing on this transaction, I am afraid and embarrassed to disclose my profit in this book because it was ridiculous. This is how the banks get rich in this America. I always tell people getting started in any business and want to get rich " you must first understand money before you could get rich" I study how all these investing bankers and institutions made their money on wall street with selling whole loans.

Will because of Dodd franks a person like myself could no longer invest in these types of non performing notes unless you are lender or maybe 3 or less transaction over a period of time. The banks cut out small time investors like myself.

No worries by the time they changed the rules I have locked up ten non- performing loans. Yes I lost money as well because of the note wasn't no good or lack a broken chain of assignment of mortgage. Very risky business.

I have a friend that is ex-police officer that buys $30,000 homes to rent out. The last count I believe he told me that he just purchase his 42nd property. Crazy, crazy he spends 7 days a week tracking down rent payments, fixing these houses and always in a rush. This is a way a lot of real estate investors believe this must be accomplished to make money in real estate. I am here to tell you the opposite. Remember what I stated to make money you must first understand the way money works.

I like investors like my friend that owns 42 rental properties why? Part of my biggest business is evictions. In one of the counties in Florida in November 2016 there were over 600 evictions filed.

That's the major problems with owning rentals, is worrying about receiving your rent payment on time and the maintenance. If you have a mortgage payment on top of that property it may be difficult to make payments each month.

It's not fun tracking down tenants for payments or receiving calls at anytime. One thing I learned as an property manager tenants have no sense of time. I have received calls on Christmas Eve to replace the light bulb in the kitchen - no it's not funny at all.

If you really want to be a successful real estate investor look at what these big hedge funds and REITS are doing. They understand real estate investing. Look around you, in your area, any place in this country.

Here's the smart way of investing, purchase a commercial plot of land and build a strip mall, it really not expensive. You are just putting up a shell that's it. The tenants would ask you or their contractor to build out the unit. Think about it Subway, Insurance companies, fast food store, pool supply and any other anchor business that you could rent to. Remember these leases are 5 to 10 years. You not running around all over town tracking down you rent payments instead you are collecting big rent checks from business. I know a investor that purchase a warehouse and rent out spaces within the warehouse - smart investing, he gets it.

Here's another way, why not buy a 30 -100 unit apartment building, in my opinion is the very best investment. Remember rent increase every year and that's just one of the good benefits about a multi units apartment building. It's all cash net investment, so what if one or two people are late you could still make your mortgage payment, think about the tax advantage.

Speaking about financing, it's is much easier to obtain financing for any of these projects mention than residential property. I would rather arrange financing for a commercial project than a residential home simply because less regulation. Dodd franks demands too many regulations on a home purchase even the lenders are not in control.

I once received a loan condition on a client loan because on the Purchase contract it had Terr. written on it. I asked the underwriter why they condition me for something that sounds so silly. After she explain to me it made perfect sense. Here the reason for the condition if the purchase agreement is writing with a address such 123 Main Terr. The purchaser could submit a claim that this isn't their correct address so we had to get a Addendum to the contract to write out the complete address to reflect 123 Main Terrace - crazy right? Well not really, they are multiple claims out there that people will try to use to take full advantage of. Remember if you have to go in front of a judge, the judge give more weight to the tenant or homeowner, you're the big bad wolf, you would have to wait for your money.

I had once had client reach out to us about a eviction, this tenant haven't paid rent in 6 months because the tenant convinced the judge that they were unable to find a job and another place to rent because of health issues. This poor investor asked us to help them short sale the property because they couldn't keep up the rent payments. The homeowner submitted all the eviction court paperwork themselves in a effort to save money, by the time they came to us the only direction was to short sale the property.

The one thing if you are renting, inside your homeowner policy you do have the option to obtain rent loss insurance, It's simply a additional rider that you could purchase. This little fact would had save this homeowners, the policy would had kick in and pay a portion of the rent and all legal fees.

This is the reason it's important to work with a expert . This small advise could had save their property. When our firm is handling the property management we would ALWAYS advise the client to purchase rent loss coverage rider. It's only a few dollars more but worth it. Most investors have never heard of this before but most major insurance companies offer this rider.

I experience good and the mostly the bad in real estate investing, my goal is to purchase a multi units apartment complex, by far it's the most effective investment and could also be handed down to the family and keep them intact for years to come.

The real estate market changes, at some point it's a seller market and then it reverse to a buyers market. The most stable market in my opinion without a doubt has to be commercial.

But like always the most important thing when investing in real estate is location, location, location.

I had a real estate agent called me out of the blue wanting to sell me his property at a heavy discount, a great deal until I asked him the address - that would explained the extreme discount. I had to decline even though I could had flip it and made a profit, but I understood it would be some serious hold time before I could find a buyer. Time is money in the real estate business, and I always will tell sellers of this. I would have to worry about the vandalism to the property, people moving in without permission- a major headache.

When you are planning on buying real estate and using it as a investment tool surround yourself around a expert Realtor that understand Cap rates, dept/income ratios, provide profit loss statement, property management. Don't waste your time with a realtor that don't understand this concepts of investing, you could end up losing a lot of money. You are investing to make money not to lose your pants.

Would you go to a foot doctor if you have chest pains? No you want a cardiac specialist . It the same when you are dealing with your money involving real estate.

It really upset me when we receive calls from clients when it's really too late in the game to save their property. By getting bad advise - is it really the person giving you the bad advice or were you just a little bit lazy to do the research on what is your biggest investment?

Always work with a expert, when dealing with your biggest investment!